SHAPEDBY**SCRIPTURE**

Consider It Pure Joy

JAMES

C. JEANNE ORJALA SERRÃO

Contents

Introduction to the *Shaped by Scripture* Series   4

Introduction to the Book of James   7

Week One: Joyful in Trials (James 1:1–11)   14

Week Two: Temptation and Pure Religion (James 1:12–27)   25

Week Three: Favoritism (James 2:1–13)   41

Week Four: Faith and Actions (James 2:14–26)   53

Week Five: Controlling the Tongue (James 3)   67

Week Six: Human Desire (James 4)   81

Week Seven: Life in Community (James 5)   96

THE *SHAPED BY SCRIPTURE* SERIES

The first step of an organized study of the Bible is the selection of a biblical book, which is not always an easy task. Often people pick a book they are already familiar with, books they think will be easy to understand, or books that, according to popular opinion, seem to have more relevance to Christians today than other books of the Bible. However, it is important to recognize the truth that God's Word is not limited to just a few books. All the biblical books, both individually and collectively, communicate God's Word to us. As Paul affirms in 2 Timothy 3:16, "All Scripture is God-breathed and is useful for teaching, rebuking, correcting and training in righteousness." We interpret the term "God-breathed" to mean inspired by God. If Christians are going to take 2 Timothy 3:16 seriously, then we should all set the goal of encountering God's Word as communicated through all sixty-six books of the Bible. New Christians or those with little to no prior knowledge of the Bible might find it best to start with a New Testament book like 1 John, James, or the Gospel of John.

By purchasing this volume, you have chosen to study the book of James. You have made a great choice because James teaches us that our faith is lived out in what we do. The goal of this series is to illustrate an appropriate method of studying the Bible. Since James is a short, five-chapter book, it is a perfect size for in-depth Bible study.

How This Study Works

This Bible study is intended for a period of seven weeks. We have chosen a specific passage for each week's study. This study can be done individually or with a small group.

For individual study, we recommend a five-day study each week, following the guidelines given below:

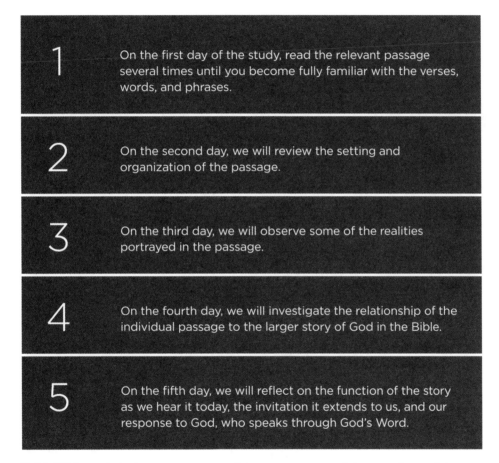

1 On the first day of the study, read the relevant passage several times until you become fully familiar with the verses, words, and phrases.

2 On the second day, we will review the setting and organization of the passage.

3 On the third day, we will observe some of the realities portrayed in the passage.

4 On the fourth day, we will investigate the relationship of the individual passage to the larger story of God in the Bible.

5 On the fifth day, we will reflect on the function of the story as we hear it today, the invitation it extends to us, and our response to God, who speaks through God's Word.

If this Bible study is done as a group activity, we recommend that members of the group meet together on the sixth day to share and discuss what they have learned from God's Word and how it has transformed their lives.

Literary Forms in the Bible

There are several literary forms represented throughout the Bible. The divinely inspired writers used various techniques to communicate God's Word to their ancient audiences. The major literary forms (also known as genres) of the Bible are:

- narratives

- laws

- history

- Wisdom literature (in the form of dialogues and proverbial statements)

- poetry (consisting of poems of praise, lament, trust in God, and more)

- prophecy

- discourses

- parables

- miracle stories

- letters (also known as epistles)

- exhortations

- apocalyptic writings

Within each of these forms, one may find subgenres. Each volume in the *Shaped by Scripture* series will briefly overview the genres found in the book of the Bible that is the subject of that study.

When biblical writers utilized a particular literary form, they intended for it to have a specific effect on their audience. This concept can be understood by examining genres that are familiar to us in our contemporary setting. For example, novels that are comedies inspire good and happy feelings in their readers; tragedies, on the other hand, are meant to induce sorrow. What is true of the intended effect of literary forms in contemporary literature is also true of literary forms found in the Bible.

THE BOOK OF JAMES

The message of the biblical books, though it originates with God, comes to us through individuals whom God inspired to communicate his word to humanity. They fulfilled their task by utilizing their literary skill as speakers and writers of God's message. This message came to these individuals in particular circumstances in the history of God's people—the Israelites in the Old Testament period, and the Christian church in the first century AD. In addition, biblical books communicate certain clearly developed understandings about God, humanity, sin, judgment, salvation, human hope, and more. Bible studies should be done with an awareness of the theological themes in a particular book. So, prior to our engagement with the actual text of James, we will briefly summarize what we know about the book in general, the authorship of James, literary forms found in the book, the historical setting of the book and that of its writing, and its major theological themes.

General Epistles

The book of James belongs to a collection of eight books (Hebrews, James, 1 & 2 Peter, 1, 2, & 3 John, and Jude) known as the general, or "catholic" (i.e., universal) epistles or letters. Some put Hebrews in a class by itself, since some ancient authors assigned Paul as its author even though consensus now is that we don't know who wrote Hebrews, thus making James the first in the list of general epistles.

These books are called "general" epistles because they were written to groups of churches or to the church universal. They also offer an alternative voice to the apostle Paul's letters on issues of belief and practice. It is important to study all the biblical voices, since Christianity was founded and spread by more people than just the apostle Paul and his coworkers.

The general epistles are strongly influenced by their Jewish roots, so they emphasize the importance of actions, which are the practical demonstrations of faith. In first-century Jewish thinking and in the thinking of these Jewish-Christian writers, there is no division in a person between what they truly believe and the actions of their lives. So one could say they believed something, but unless their actions bore out that belief, what they said didn't matter much.

Some have said that James contradicts Paul's gospel of faith and grace because of James's emphasis on works. But if one reads both authors carefully, it is obvious that Paul emphasizes in his exhortations (which appear in every one of his letters) how we should live in light of our faith and the grace that God has extended to us. In the same way, James does not discount faith or grace but emphasizes that, if one truly has faith, it will become apparent in how one acts and treats others. The best way to describe the relationship between James and Paul is complementary. James emphasizes the outward aspects of faith, and Paul emphasizes the inward aspects of faith.

Who Wrote James?

The authorship of the book of James has been debated from the early centuries of Christianity. There are several people named "James" in the New Testament, including the son of Zebedee (Mark 1:19), the son of Alphaeus (Mark 3:18), the brother of Jesus (Mark 6:3), the younger (Mark 15:40), and the father of Judas (not Iscariot, Luke 6:16). All of these people have been discounted as the author of James for various reasons except for the brother of Jesus, who was a recognized leader of Jewish Christians, being one of the main conveners of the Jerusalem Council in AD 49 (see Acts 15).

The main issue for the authorship debate is the fact that the book of James was written in excellent first-century Greek. If we assign the authorship to James—Jesus's Galilean brother—it seems unlikely that he would have had the necessary education and writing skills. The solutions have suggested that James was later edited by a skilled Greek scholar, or that James was written by an anonymous person who used James's name to indicate the theological tradition in which he was writing. Though authorship of James and many other biblical books is frequently debated among Christians, we believe in the integrity of biblical books as we find them in the Bible today.

Literary Form

The book of James begins like a traditional Greco-Roman letter with a salutation that names both the sender and the receiver of the letter, but it does not have the typical prayer or words of thanksgiving that we find, for example, in Paul's letters. Nor does it have a regular ending with greetings or a benediction. It is clearly a well-crafted piece of literature intended for a wide audience of Jewish Christians. But it is not an informal or personal letter.

The body of this letter can be described as a sermon that uses subgenres of Wisdom literature. James's purpose was to teach the readers how to live, which is one of the most common themes of Wisdom literature in the Old Testament. The author does this through debates that have the technical name of "diatribe" (taking on the archaic meaning of a prolonged discourse, rather than the overtly negative meaning that modern definitions of this word employ today). Synagogue sermons often used the diatribe format, consisting of a series of questions and answers with an imaginary debate partner. We find this style most evident in James 2 in the discussion of the themes of faith and action ("works"). Another subgenre of Wisdom literature found in James is sayings, or proverbs. James often states a proverb and then teaches his lesson based on it.

The Wisdom Genres

The technical name for the rhetorical (or speechlike) style used in James is *paraenesis*. What this scholarly word means is that the purpose of James was to encourage readers to remember what they had already been taught. The author did not expect to be telling his readers anything new. Perhaps James was concerned that his audience was too influenced by Greek thinking, which meant they thought that all they needed to do was accept the grace of God and have faith in God's Son. In this letter James is calling readers to act according to their faith.

Historical Context

As with the authorship of James, there is debate on the date of the writing. Those who think the author was anonymous put the date in the second century AD (100s). Those who think it was James the brother of Jesus put the date between AD 40 and 49, before the Jerusalem Council. If it seems likely that an editor was needed to put this book in excellent Greek, the date for the editing is usually put in the first half of the second century.

This letter does reflect the historical setting of what we know of Jerusalem and the surrounding area during the first century. There was much political and social instability, famines, and periods of anarchy between appointments of Roman governors. As we know from history, instability and economic problems especially affect the poor. We see deep concern for the poor reflected in James, indicating at times that the audience may have been poor but also, at other times, instructing the audience to help the poor.

There is also emphasis on how Christians should live, reflected in the admonition to control the tongue and be aware of where temptations come from. For James, temptations come from our own desires; there is no "the devil made me do it" rationale here. In addition, while James may be addressing the poor on issues of desire, he also has strong words for the rich in chapter 5 because of their oppression of the poor.

Structure And Organization

Like authorship and date, the structure of James is also debated, primarily because of the book's proverbial nature. One structural concept that most can agree on is that chapter 1 is an abstract or outline of the whole book. It contains most of the major themes that James goes on to cover in the rest of the book.

The theme of James is salvation by obedient faith—we are to "not merely listen to the word," but we are also meant to "do what it says" (1:22). Themes of wisdom, perseverance, and the identification of Christians with the righteous poor are found in chapter 1. At the end of the first chapter, we find the only place in the New Testament that defines religion. The term James uses is one that indicates the outward actions of religion: "to look after orphans and widows in their distress and to keep oneself from being polluted by the world" (v. 27). Here we see the unity between the gospel of purity and the social gospel of compassion.

Chapters 2–5, while thought by some to have no particular order, do seem to be organized into a group of units that appear to have typical Greek openings and closings. The nature of these units are exhortations or strong encouragements and instructions on how to live a life that pleases God.

10

The second unit (2:1–13) begins with the issues of showing favoritism and is of special concern for James since it violates the royal law, "Love your neighbor as yourself" (v. 8). From this exposition and example he moves to the famous "faith and works" section (2:14–26). Here he says, "I will show you my faith by my deeds" (v. 18). He then goes on to show that Abraham and Rahab were considered righteous by what they did.

The third unit (3:1–12) moves to a specific way people reveal who they really are—by what they say. Interestingly, James begins with teachers—an identity of people who were greatly respected in the first century—and the fact that they will be judged more harshly than others by what they say. Then he moves to the idea that the tongue is so uncontrollable that nothing and no one on earth can tame it. This tongue both praises God and curses those who were made in the image of God. This situation is clearly not as it should be, and only God can help us!

The fourth unit (3:13–18) contrasts earthly and heavenly wisdom.

In the fifth unit (4:1–10), James moves back to an idea he talked about in the third section, where he characterized those who both bless God and curse God's image as "double-minded." Here he builds on this idea, bringing in the idea of desire from the first chapter as the original root of sin. James tells his audience that this state of double-mindedness—or trying to be friends with the world and with God—is impossible to maintain. One must humble oneself, repent, and then find God's forgiveness.

With unit six, James begins a series of short reminders of how one is to live as a Christian. First, we are not to judge our neighbor (4:11–12) because God is both the Lawgiver and the Judge. Secondly, we are not to make plans for the future without taking the will of God into consideration (vv. 13–17). We do not know what will happen tomorrow, and furthermore, our lives in comparison to the grand scheme of God are like steam that appears over a boiling pot for a little while and then disappears!

In chapter 5 (vv. 1–6), James warns the rich who have gotten their wealth through the oppression of the poor to repent because their punishment is sure to come. Then he turns to the poor (vv. 7–11) and encourages them to have patience because the Lord is coming soon and will bring justice. Here he returns to the theme of perseverance or endurance and brings in Job as an example.

The last three units have to do with life in the church community. We are called to simple truthfulness as we relate to others (5:12). There should be no need to swear by anything to convince another person we are being truthful. We are to pray with those who are suffering and be happy and sing with those who are cheerful. Those who are sick should call for the elders of the church to anoint them with oil and pray for them (vv. 13–18). Finally, the community is to have compassion on the brother or sister who wanders from the truth (vv. 19–20).

This church community truly loves and cares for one another! Our plan is to study this book to discover the secrets of a loving and caring church community.

Major Theological Themes

While James is primarily concerned with the practical issues of how a Christian should live, these discussions reflect some significant theological themes. The following list will give a sense of the theological framework of James.

God, the Creator and the source of all gifts—especially wisdom, is a dependable and righteous judge; he gives grace to all who endure suffering.

The Lord Jesus Christ is Lord, Messiah, and God. Jesus is the *shekinah* glory of God, the manifestation of the personal presence of *Yahweh*.

Salvation is not through good actions or works, but good actions and works do come as a result of salvation. There is a close relationship between physical healing and spiritual salvation.

God's law is perfect and brings freedom. It is summarized as "Love your neighbor as yourself." It is relational and not legalistic.

The Word gives us life. While there is a close relationship between the law and the Word, only the implanted Word can save.

Trials are ordinary troubles that every person has, while temptations come because of our desires. God sends neither, but they can bring about personal and spiritual maturity.

Wealth and poverty are turned upside down in James. The poor or humble are highly regarded; the rich are not.

Faith comes before good works, but good works are a necessary outcome of faith. Faith without good works is dead or worthless.

 God-given wisdom promotes peace and harmony, while earthly wisdom promotes jealously, rivalry, confusion, and worthless practices.

 The tongue is so difficult to control that only God can control our speech.

 Prayer is both a personal and corporate activity. We are to pray for one another and should not be ashamed to ask God for anything.

 Salvation affects the whole person, bringing transformation to our mental, spiritual, emotional, and physical dimensions. Wholeness also has to do with the community, so we pray for wholeness in our church community.

 The end times will bring about justice. Readers are to be patient because "the Lord's coming is near" (5:8).

JAMES 1:1–11

Our purpose in studying the first eleven verses of James is to reflect on why perseverance in testing is so important to becoming mature Christians, why we are to ask God for wisdom, and why Christians should be humble, no matter what level of respect they have in the community.

These first eleven verses are the first half of James's overview or introduction to the instructions he is giving these first-century church communities. He touches on the most important topics that he will be coming back to and developing in chapters 2–5.

Scholars have noted the following pattern in the organization of these verses:

1. Salutation, or greeting ("James, a servant of God . . . To the twelve tribes . . .").

2. Trials and temptations ("Consider it pure joy . . . whenever you face trials . . .").

3. Ask for wisdom ("If any of you lacks wisdom . . . ask God . . .").

4. Believers are humble ("Believers in humble circumstances . . . take pride in their high position . . .").

14

WEEK 1, DAY 1

Absorb the passage in James 1:1–11 by reading it aloud several times until you become familiar with its verses, words, and phrases. Enjoy hearing the heart of James as he begins his message to his readers.

WEEK 1, DAY 2

JAMES 1:1–11

The Setting

It is customary to begin the study of a biblical passage by asking questions about its historical, cultural, religious, and literary setting. James is a Jewish Christian writing to fellow Jewish Christians in the first century. These Jewish Christians are subjects of the polytheistic and pagan Roman Empire. They are most likely living outside of Israel in cities where they are the minority. Some may have grown up in these cities, but their lifestyle and customs are noticeably different from those of their neighbors. James uses the normal method of that time of communicating across distances through writing a letter.

The traditional date for the writing of this letter is between AD 40 and 62. During this time, James was the leader of the church in Jerusalem and served as a kind of bishop of the Jewish Christians. In AD 49 he moderated the Council of Jerusalem, which was called because of the tremendous response of gentiles to the gospel during the first missionary journey of Paul and Barnabas. He agreed with Paul and Peter that gentiles should not have to become Jews to be Christians.

The Message

To discover the message of James 1:1–11, let us examine the passage verse by verse, essentially dividing it into eleven sections. **Below, summarize or paraphrase the general message or theme of each verse (following the pattern provided for verses 1, 2, and 11).**

1. James 1:1

James is a servant of God and of Jesus Christ, and he is writing to Jewish Christians who are living outside of Jerusalem.

2. James 1:2

We are to consider trials as something to be happy about.

3. James 1:3

_____

_____

4. James 1:4

_____

_____

5. James 1:5

_____

_____

6. James 1:6

_____

_____

7. James 1:7

_____

_____

8. James 1:8

_____

_____

9. James 1:9

_____

_____

10. James 1:10

_____

_____

11. James 1:11
The earthly significance of the wealthy or proud will not last forever.

_____

WEEK 1, DAY 3

What's Happening in the Passage?

As we notice certain emphases in the passage, we will begin to see how they are similar to or different from the realities of our world. The passage will become the lens through which we see the world in which we live today. In our study today, you may encounter words and/or phrases that are unfamiliar to you. Some of the particular words and translation choices for them have been explained in more detail in the **Word Study Notes**. If you are interested in even more help or detail, you can supplement this study with a Bible dictionary or other Bible study resource.

1. James 1:1

This letter begins by identifying the writer as James, who considers himself a servant[1] of God and of Jesus Christ. He is writing to the "twelve tribes" who live in the Roman Empire outside of Jerusalem.[2]

2. James 1:2

James anticipates that his readers will experience unexpected trials.[1] Although joy is not the natural human response, they need to learn as Christians to receive all kinds of trials with joy.

17

WORD STUDY NOTES #1

[1] The word translated as "servant" is the same word used to mean "slave." This low status group is identified not by their parents or occupation but by whom they serve. Because of the context of this letter, this identification has a dual meaning of both identifying the author as humble but also to put him in the same category as Moses, who was a servant of God (Numbers 12:7).

[2] The identification of the readers as those who are "scattered among the nations" actually uses the technical term of "dispersion," or "Diaspora," which indicates that these Jewish Christians are not living in the traditionally Jewish areas of Judea and Galilee. They are most likely living in Greco-Roman cities and have noticeably different customs than their neighbors, which would cause them to need wisdom on how to live. It also indicates that they could be socially persecuted or ostracized by their neighbors who do not understand their customs.

WORD STUDY NOTES #2

[1] The Greek word translated "trials" here can mean trials *or* temptations. The Greek tense used for the verb "consider" means to *begin* to consider. James recognizes that seeing trials as something to be joyful about is an attitude that must be learned.

WORD STUDY NOTES #3

[1] The Greek word translated "testing" here is a different word from the one for trials or temptations. This word indicates the *process* of testing.

WORD STUDY NOTES #4

[1] The word translated "mature" in the NIV can also be translated "perfect." This important word is also found in 1:17, "perfect gift;" in 1:25, "perfect law;" and in 3:2, "perfect one." It is used in the Hebrew sense of fulfilling one's purpose rather than the Greek sense (and our Western cultural understanding) of flawlessness.

3. James 1:3

The reason we learn to receive trials with joy is that, in the process of dealing with trials, we develop perseverance in our character.[1]

Practice the above pattern to summarize the reality that is portrayed in verse 4.

4. James 1:4[1]

_____

_____

_____

_____

_____

5. James 1:5

Christians can ask God daily for wisdom, knowing they will not be shamed by God for asking and that God will give the wisdom needed.

6. James 1:6

When a person does ask God for wisdom, they must be ready to act on that wisdom and not doubt God. Those who doubt God are like a wave in the middle of the ocean that goes wherever the wind blows. It has no purpose or direction, and other forces direct where it goes.

7. James 1:7

Response from God comes when one is completely committed to and has faith in God.

Create your own brief summary or description of the reality portrayed in verse 8.

8. James 1:8[1]

_____

_____

_____

_____

_____

9. James 1:9

The poor or humble have a high position with God because they understand that they need God in their lives.

10. James 1:10[1]

_____

_____

_____

_____

_____

11. James 1:11

Here James uses a proverb from nature to describe the life of the rich person. While they may rise to great heights and look really good for a while, their earthly lives are worth nothing and will eventually pass away.

WORD STUDY NOTES #8

[1] The word translated "double-minded" means, literally, "two-souled." While this particular word is not found elsewhere in Greek literature before the epistle of James, the idea of two souls is found in Jewish traditional literature in commands that instruct believers not to come to God with a divided mind or heart.

WORD STUDY NOTES #10

[1] First-century people believed that the limitedness of resources meant that, if someone had more than was needed, they had taken what rightfully belonged to others. Therefore, the rich, by definition, were considered evil. Also, during the Syrian empire persecution about 160 years before Jesus was born, the poor were the ones who stood up to the Syrians, while the rich saw economic advantage in assimilating and cooperating with the Syrians. So the idea of the poor being righteous had carried over into first-century Jewish culture and thinking.

Discoveries

Let's summarize our discoveries from James 1:1–11.

1. As Christians, we should be identified by whom we serve: the Lord Jesus Christ.

2. All Christians will have unexpected trials in life, which they can learn to experience with joy because they know these will help them develop character and grow in faith.

3. As we encounter life, we have access to the full wisdom of God. All we have to do is ask and be willing to act on what God says to us.

4. Those who doubt God are trying to live in two worlds—one in which they follow their own desires and one in which they follow God's will. They will never be able to move forward in their lives with God.

5. Those who live for themselves might look good, but their lives are shallow and leave nothing of value when they are gone.

WEEK 1, DAY 4

Joyful in Trials and the Story of God

Whenever we read a biblical text, it is important to ask how the particular text we are reading relates to the rest of the Bible. The themes of being joyful in trials and asking for wisdom from God have an important place in the story of God. These themes are found in several other places in the Bible in a variety of contexts.

In the Old and New Testaments, the themes of trials that produce character and asking God for wisdom are numerous. Often the idea of the effect of trials uses the metaphor of smelting ore to produce the pure silver or gold metals. Of course, the most famous person to ask God for wisdom was King Solomon.

Places in the Old Testament where these themes are notably present include but are not limited to 1 Kings 3:5–12; Psalm 66:1–2, 8–12; Proverbs 9:10–12; and Isaiah 40:27–31. **In the space given below, write a short summary of how the trial and wisdom themes are utilized in each passage.**

1 Kings 3:5–12

_____

_____

_____

_____

Psalm 66:1–2, 8–12

_____

_____

_____

_____

If you have a study Bible, it may have references in a margin, a middle column, or footnotes that point to other biblical texts. You may find it helpful in understanding how the whole story of God ties together to look up some of those other scriptures from time to time.

Proverbs 9:10–12

_____

_____

_____

_____

Isaiah 40:27–31

_____

_____

_____

_____

We also see these themes elsewhere in the New Testament, in the context of the work of salvation that God accomplished through Jesus Christ. **In the space given below, write a short summary of how the themes of trial and wisdom are utilized in the following passages.**

Matthew 5:10–12

_____

_____

_____

_____

Colossians 2:2–5

_____

_____

_____

_____

2 Thessalonians 1:3–7

_____

_____

_____

_____

WEEK 1, DAY 5

James and Our World Today

When we look at the themes of trial and wisdom in James 1:1–11, they can become the lens through which we see ourselves, our world, and how God works in our world today.

1. What do we see when we look at ourselves and our world through the lens of James's perspective of rejoicing in trials?

Many people, including Christians, do not respond to troubles and trials with joy. Bitterness and complaint are much more common. It's more difficult to think of trials as opportunities to experience God's presence with us and develop character.

Following the above example, answer these questions about how we can understand ourselves, our world, and God's action in our world today.

2. What do you observe about those around you who have gone through difficult times when seen through the lens of this text?

3. We often desire to protect the children in our lives from difficult times (even if they aren't our own children). What does this theme of learning to rejoice in trials and the importance of developing character say to us about how we should be talking to the children in our lives about things that are hard?

4. How do you see godly wisdom differing from earthly wisdom in your life?

_____

_____

_____

_____

_____

5. James encourages us to ask for wisdom daily and then to be ready to do what God says without hesitation. What is the world's attitude about this way of life?

_____

_____

_____

_____

_____

Invitation and Response

God's Word always invites a response. Think about the way these themes of trials and wisdom from James 1:1–11 speak to us today. How do they invite us to respond?

When we go through trials in our lives, God's Word invites us to trust in God's presence with us and consider the opportunities to develop character. God's Word also invites us to follow the examples of those who have trusted in God's presence and developed character when they went through trials.

_____

_____

What is your evaluation of yourself based on any or all of the verses found in James 1:1–11?

_____

_____

_____

_____

JAMES 1:12-27

The purpose of our study of James 1:12–27 is to discover the roles of temptation, anger, listening, and doing in our lives, and to discover what is true or pure religion. This seems like a lot of stuff for a few short verses, but that is the nature of Wisdom and proverbial literature. Many important ideas are packed into these verses that James will proceed to unpack in the following four chapters.

Scholars have noted the following pattern in the organization of these verses:

1. God does not tempt us ("God cannot be tempted . . . nor does he tempt anyone").

2. Be slow to get angry ("Everyone should be quick to listen . . . and slow to become angry").

3. Listen and act ("Do not merely listen to the word . . . Do what it says").

4. Pure religion ("Religion that God our Father accepts . . . to look after orphans and widows . . . and to keep oneself from being polluted . . .").

WEEK 2, DAY 1

Absorb the passage in James 1:12–27 by reading it aloud several times until you become familiar with its verses, words, and phrases. Enjoy hearing the heart of James as he continues summarizing his message to his readers.

WEEK 2, DAY 2

JAMES 1:12-27

The Setting

This passage is the second half of the first chapter of James in which the author is summarizing his message to his readers. There are several ideas that the original audience would have understood that are basic to understanding these verses today. First, James, like Paul, sees the Christian life as a race in which those who persevere to the end will win a prize. In the first century, this prize was a laurel wreath, often referred to as a crown.

Second, it was popular among first-century Jews to believe that God was responsible for everything that happened in a person's life. James challenges this belief, saying that God is the one who gives good gifts but that temptations and bad things that happen to people are the result of their own desires. He places the blame for evil on the individual, not on Satan or God.

The wisdom of being quick to listen and slow to speak is part of a broader wisdom tradition found in both Greek and Jewish philosophers and writers. The idea that anger is destructive is also found in both traditions.

James refers to his audience in this section as hearers rather than readers because the first-century culture was an oral one. James expected the letter to be read aloud to a church community, rather than each individual in the community reading the letter for themselves.

The term "religion" used in this passage is a Greek word that refers to external religious practices. This was the common way to identify a person's religion in the first century. The pagan gentiles gave offerings to the gods in their many temples while the Jews observed their purity and dietary laws. James believes that Christianity also has external practices that identify the Christian.

The Message

To discover the message of James 1:12–27, let's divide this passage into eleven sections. **Summarize or paraphrase the general message or theme of each verse or grouping of verses (following the pattern provided for verses 12, 13, and 27).**

1. James 1:12

Those who persevere in living the Christian life will receive the crown of everlasting life.

_____

_____

_____

_____

_____

_____

2. James 1:13

Temptation does not come from God. God cannot be tempted and does not tempt anyone.

_____

_____

_____

_____

_____

_____

3. James 1:14–15

_____

_____

_____

_____

_____

_____

4. James 1:16–17

_____

_____

_____

_____

_____

_____

5. James 1:18

_____

_____

_____

_____

_____

_____

6. James 1:19–21

_____

_____

_____

_____

_____

_____

7. James 1:22

_____

_____

_____

_____

_____

_____

8. James 1:23–24

_____

_____

_____

_____

_____

_____

9. James 1:25

_____

_____

_____

_____

_____

_____

10. James 1:26

_____

_____

_____

_____

_____

_____

11. James 1:27
You can tell who is a true Christian by their compassionate care and attitude of giving to those on the margins and by the fact that they live Christlike, pure lives.

_____

_____

_____

WEEK 2, DAY 3

What's Happening in the Passage?

As we notice certain emphases in the passage, we will begin to see how they are similar to or different from the realities of our world. The passage will become the lens through which we see the world in which we live today. In our study today, you may encounter words and/or phrases that are unfamiliar to you. Some of the particular words and translation choices for them have been explained in more detail in the **Word Study Notes**. If you are interested in even more help or detail, you can supplement this study with a Bible dictionary or other Bible study resource.

1. James 1:12

James begins this section by restating the fact that all Christians will face trials. They must persevere, and when they do, they will receive the crown[1] of life that God has promised to those who love him. This is the prize of everlasting life.

2. James 1:13

Temptation comes to everyone, but God is not the source of temptation. God is not able to be tempted and does not tempt anyone.[1] James is adamant here that God is not the source of our temptations or trials.

WORD STUDY NOTES #1

[1] The word translated "crown" is the term used in Greek life and culture for the reward athletes won as they persevered in their competitions (a culturally equivalent word today might be "trophy" or "ribbon" or even simply "prize"). In Greek life, the crown was usually a laurel wreath.

WORD STUDY NOTES #2

[1] The verb translated here as "being tempted" is from the same root as the word for "trials." The Greek root can mean trial or temptation, but in this transitional verse it is becoming obvious that James is referring to the temptation to sin, not just an unexpected problem that happens in life.

3. James 1:14–15

People are seduced by their desires,[1] and when they give in to their desires, sin[2] is conceived in their hearts. Moreover, sin, when it is acted upon, gives birth to spiritual death.

Practice the above pattern to summarize the reality portrayed in verses 16–17.

4. James 1:16–17[1, 2]

_____

_____

_____

_____

_____

5. James 1:18

This verse is the opposite parallel of verse 15. Here God, after he wills it,[1] gives birth[2] to us by the word of truth. As human beings, we are the crown of his creation.

6. James 1:19-21

We are to be continually[1] listening to others, to really hear what they are saying. Then, when we understand, we can speak with wisdom and not fall prey to deep-seated anger.[2] Human anger rarely produces righteousness, so we are to rid ourselves of the immorality and hatred that are so much a part of our world. God's Word can become part of who we are, and it is by God's Word that we are made whole—that we are saved.

7. James 1:22

We must continue to do what God's Word says and not just hear it. If we never act on what God's Word tells us to do, we do not understand the nature of the gospel.

Create your own brief summary or description of the reality portrayed in verses 23-24.

8. James 1:23-24[1]

_____

_____

_____

_____

_____

9. James 1:25

Whoever studies intently the perfect law of God—which brings freedom and instruction on how we should live—*and* does what it says will be blessed.[1]

WORD STUDY NOTES #6

[1] These verses begin with a continuous command: "Know this," or "continue to be aware of this!" Therefore, what follows is something of which we need to be constantly aware.

[2] The word translated "anger" is one of three words for anger in ancient Greek. One, found in Ephesians 4:26, is a common, sudden emotion that arises from frustration. The other two, found in Ephesians 4:31 and translated as "rage" and "anger," are more serious forms. The word translated "rage" is also a sudden, passionate eruption of emotion, but it comes from unresolved, deeply entrenched anger, which is the word James uses here in these verses. This last strong word for anger is sometimes translated as "wrath."

WORD STUDY NOTES #8

[1] The word translated "looks" is not the simple word for "see." Instead, it is better understood as "to contemplate." So the one who looks in the mirror is contemplating himself or herself for the purpose of doing something about his or her appearance.

WORD STUDY NOTES #9

[1] The word translated "looks intently" is an even stronger word than the "look" used in verse 23. It means to "bend over" to get a closer look at something.

[1] The word translated "religion" refers to the outward expression of religion.

[2] The word translated "deceive" has the connotation of being self-absorbed—because this person's religion does not care for the needs of others.

10. James 1:26[1, 2]

_____

_____

_____

_____

11. James 1:27

Those who are truly religious will visit the marginalized and care for them in their contexts—and, at the same time, will keep themselves from being contaminated by worldly values and desires that lead to sin.

Discoveries

Let's summarize our discoveries from James 1:12–27.

1. God does not tempt us to do evil things.

2. Our own personal desires are what drag us into sinful thoughts. If we act on our sinful thoughts, they become sinful acts and result in spiritual death.

3. No one is exempt from temptation, but God is interested in giving each of us what we need to persevere in the middle of temptation.

4. There is status and reward for those who persevere and love God!

5. We are instructed to listen intently, speak carefully, and avoid anger because human anger does not produce Christlike qualities in our lives.

6. We deceive ourselves if we think it is enough just to listen to or "believe in" God's Word. We have to act on it.

7. God's Word was given to us to make a difference in our lives and in the lives of those around us.

WEEK 2, DAY 4

Temptation, Pure Religion, and the Story of God

If you have a study Bible, it may have references in a margin, a middle column, or footnotes that point to other biblical texts. You may find it helpful in understanding how the whole story of God ties together to look up some of those other scriptures from time to time. Whenever we read a biblical text, it is important to ask how the particular text we are reading relates to the rest of the Bible. The themes surrounding the nature of temptation and pure religion have an important place in the story of God. These themes are found in several places in the Bible in a variety of contexts.

In the Old and New Testaments, these themes are common. The prophets often called out the people who thought they were religious but lived totally for themselves.

Places where these themes are notably present include but are not limited to the scriptures listed below. **Write a short summary of how the themes of temptation and/or pure religion (living the right way as a person of God) are utilized in these scriptures.**

Leviticus 19:18

_____

_____

_____

_____

_____

_____

Proverbs 11:6

_____

_____

_____

_____

_____

_____

Micah 6:6–8

_____

_____

_____

_____

_____

_____

Habakkuk 2:4

_____

_____

_____

_____

_____

_____

Luke 6:27–31

_____

_____

_____

_____

_____

_____

Romans 1:24–25

_____

_____

_____

_____

_____

_____

1 Corinthians 13:4–7

_____

_____

_____

_____

_____

_____

1 Peter 1:13–16

_____

_____

_____

_____

_____

_____

WEEK 2, DAY 5

James and Our World Today

When we look at the themes of temptation and pure religion in James 1:12–27, they can become the lens through which we see ourselves, our world, and how God works in our world today.

1. If we understand that the temptation to sin comes from our own desires and not from God, how does that understanding affect how we see ourselves and our world?

We know that our world offers us seemingly limitless possibilities for desire—certainly we have more opportunities to be tempted by our desires today than were available in the first century. This reality should caution us to set our own personal boundaries on what we expose ourselves to. We need God's strength and wisdom as much as or more than those first hearers of James's letter did.

Following the above example, answer these questions about how we can understand ourselves, our world, and God's action in our world today.

2. What do you observe about the targeted marketing we are subjected to by social media and how it affects our desires?

_____

_____

_____

_____

_____

3. If God wants to reward us for resisting temptation, and is interested in helping us bear our temptations, how can we take advantage of that relationally with God?

_____

_____

_____

_____

_____

4. James teaches us that we can be recognized as Christians (and can practice "pure religion") by our outward actions toward those who live on the margins of our society. What outward actions mark you as a Christian?

_____

_____

_____

_____

_____

5. Since we are encouraged by James to get out into the world and serve the world but are also told to maintain our own purity of mind and heart, how do we do both at the same time?

_____

_____

_____

_____

_____

Invitation and Response

God's Word always invites a response. Think about the way these themes of temptation and pure religion from James 1:12–27 speak to us today. How do they invite us to respond?

James invites us to consider intentional ways we can be better listeners and slower to become angry in certain situations. James also asks us to examine our hearts and motivations to see whether the actions, rhythms, and patterns of our lives line up with the Word of God.

What is your evaluation of yourself based on any or all of the verses found in James 1:12–27?

_____

_____

_____

_____

God is not the source of our temptations or trials.

JAMES 2:1–13

The purpose of our study of James 2:1–13 is to discover how the issue of favoritism is a clear violation of the second great commandment of Jesus, to love our neighbors as ourselves. In chapter 2, James begins to unpack the many important ideas that he summarized in chapter 1. He begins with the issue of Christians showing favoritism based on wealth and status.

We can discern the following pattern in the organization of these verses:

1. Don't show favoritism ("My brothers and sisters, believers . . . must not show favoritism").

2. The poor are rich in faith ("Has not God chosen those who are poor . . . to be rich in faith?").

3. The law of love ("If you really keep the royal law found in Scripture, 'Love your neighbor as yourself,' you are doing right").

WEEK 3, DAY 1

Absorb the passage in James 2:1–13 by reading it aloud several times until you become familiar with its verses, words, and phrases.

WEEK 3, DAY 2

The Setting

This passage begins the body of the letter where James is putting meat on the summary bones from chapter 1. There are several ideas that the original readers would have understood that are basic to our ability to understand these verses today.

This passage encourages countercultural behavior. People of higher status expected to be treated with deference and were offended when they were not offered the best seat in the house. There was also, among Jews and Christians in the first century, a different understanding of rich and poor, as we discussed on Day 3 of Week 1. The rich—because of cultural and historical circumstances—were viewed as evil, and the poor were righteous.

Most of the readers of James in the first century, as Diaspora Jews (immigrants), would not have been citizens of the cities they lived in and were usually relatively new to the community. The wealthy status seekers in the city often sued these newcomers in court to establish superiority over them. The judges in those courts were not dispensing justice so much as delineating who had the most status or power in the community.

James picks out two of the most shocking sins of the first century. Murder was horrific because it ended the life of a person, and in the first century, adultery was more than a moral failure affecting the immediate family. The male adulterer was understood as a thief who stole the property of the husband—the fertility of his wife. This situation also made it impossible for the husband to know if the children born to his wife were actually his.

The Message

To discover the message of James 2:1–13, let us examine the passage verse by verse, dividing it into ten sections. **Summarize or paraphrase the general message or theme of each verse or grouping of verses (following the pattern provided for verses 1, 2–4, and 13).**

1. James 2:1

Believers in the resurrected Christ must not show favoritism.

2. James 2:2–4

James describes two very different people. One is filthy rich, and the other is dirt poor. The synagogue greeter shows special attention to the rich person, giving them the best seat in the house. Meanwhile the synagogue greeter tells the poor person to stand "over there" or to sit on the floor, humiliating the poor person.

3. James 2:5

4. James 2:6

5. James 2:7

6. James 2:8

_____

_____

_____

_____

_____

7. James 2:9

_____

_____

_____

_____

_____

8. James 2:10–11

_____

_____

_____

_____

_____

9. James 2:12

_____

_____

_____

_____

_____

10. James 2:13
Mercy will not be shown to those who have not been merciful.

_____

_____

_____

WEEK 3, DAY 3

What's Happening in the Passage?

As we notice the emphasis of favoritism in this passage, we will begin to see how James's first-century view is similar to or different from the realities of our world. The passage will become the lens through which we see the world in which we live today. In our study today, you may encounter words and/or phrases that are unfamiliar to you. Some of the particular words and translation choices for them have been explained in more detail in the **Word Study Notes**. If you are interested in even more help or detail, you can supplement this study with a Bible dictionary or other Bible study resource.

1. James 2:1

James begins this section by stating his thesis: Christians who have faith in the resurrected Christ[1] are not to show partiality.

2. James 2:2–4

James describes a hypothetical, exaggerated scenario in a synagogue setting. Two visitors enter the synagogue: One is obviously very wealthy with gold dripping from his fingers. The other is obviously very poor dressed in dirty, smelly rags. The reaction and actions of the greeter are obviously based on the appearances of the visitors. The wealthy person is given an honorable seat, and the poor person is humiliated by being segregated (stand "over there") or by being made to sit on the floor (a position of humiliation). The greeter has sinned by judging these visitors by their outward appearances, catering to the wealthy in hopes of gaining an advantage in society and humiliating the already-humble poor person.

WORD STUDY NOTES #1

[1] The grammar in this verse is a little difficult, so there are several ancient texts that differ as they try to clarify the original text. The best translation is "the faith of our resurrected Lord Jesus Christ," since the Greek word for "glory" is often used as shorthand for the resurrection of Jesus.

WORD STUDY NOTES #3

[1] Scholars consider this verse to be James's interpretation of the Beatitude found in Matthew 5:3, "Blessed are the poor in spirit," and in Luke 6:20, "Blessed are you who are poor."

WORD STUDY NOTES #4

[1] In the first century, family honor did not directly indicate economic status. Circumstances could result in a person being economically poor, but that did not mean they were without honor. Courts in the first century were a vehicle for the greedy and powerful to oppress those without power. As Diaspora Jews, James's readers were relatively powerless and would have been victims of the powerful. Honorable people would have settled their differences outside of court.

[2] The word translated "blaspheming" means to slander or destroy someone's reputation.

[3] The phrase translated "to whom you belong" is a good translation of the original: "the good name invoked over you." To invoke a name over someone is to claim ownership or to indicate a special relationship.

46

3. James 2:5

Remember that God chose the poor to be rich in faith and to inherit the kingdom of God.[1]

Practice the above pattern to summarize the reality that is portrayed in verses 6–7.

4. James 2:6–7[1, 2, 3]

_____

_____

_____

_____

_____

5. James 2:8

If you really live out the law[1] as interpreted by Jesus Christ, you are doing the right things.[2]

6. James 2:9

_____

_____

_____

_____

_____

7. James 2:10–11

A person can try to keep the whole law, but if they break even one rule, they are guilty of breaking the whole law.[1] God gave us both the command not to commit adultery, which means not to steal from others, and the command not to commit murder, which can also be interpreted as what you do when you do not take care of those who live on the edge of starvation.[2]

8. James 2:12[1]

_____

_____

_____

_____

_____

9. James 2:13

Those who have not shown mercy to others will not receive mercy from God. In Christ, mercy will continue to conquer judgment as witnessed in the life, death, and resurrection of Jesus.

WORD STUDY NOTES #5

[1] The term "royal law" most likely refers to the law as interpreted by Jesus Christ, but this entire passage in James 2 refers to Leviticus 19, especially verse 15, "Do not pervert justice; do not show partiality to the poor or favoritism to the great, but judge your neighbor fairly."

[2] The verb translated "keep" in this verse is not the usual one for keeping or observing the law. It is a much stronger word meaning "fulfill," "perform," or "accomplish."

WORD STUDY NOTES #7

[1] At work here is the widely held principle of the unity of the whole law. This is one reason for the development of the oral law by the Pharisees. They created laws that were more restrictive so one would not accidentally break one of the laws of the Torah.

[2] Jewish tradition associates murder with the failure to care for the poor—especially those who had no means to support themselves, like orphans and widows.

WORD STUDY NOTES #8

[1] The "law that gives freedom" is associated with the law as interpreted by Jesus Christ.

Discoveries

Let's summarize our discoveries from James 2:1–13.

1. Showing favoritism breaks the law of God because it does not treat everyone with equal dignity, and you are not loving your neighbor as you love yourself.

2. Showing favoritism for the purpose of gaining favor or position also breaks the law of God because it demonstrates judgment with evil thoughts.

3. Both Judaism and Christianity have stood with the poor, acknowledging that God has mercy on the powerless, and so should we.

4. It is difficult for the rich to recognize how their lives oppress the poor; James calls rich Christians to learn from the poor and not to expect privilege.

5. We are to live our lives according to Jesus's interpretation of the law, which requires a transformation of the person, not legalism.

6. We should learn to be merciful because God was merciful to us in sending Jesus Christ as our Savior. Those who show mercy reveal that they belong to the merciful God.

WEEK 3, DAY 4

Favoritism and the Story of God

If you have a study Bible, it may have references in a margin, a middle column, or footnotes that point to other biblical texts. You may find it helpful in understanding how the whole story of God ties together to look up some of those other scriptures from time to time. Whenever we read a biblical text, it is important to ask how the particular text we are reading relates to the rest of the Bible. The theme of not showing favoritism has an important place in the story of God. This theme is found in several places in the Bible in a variety of contexts. **In the space given below, write a short summary of how the theme of favoritism appears in each passage.**

Exodus 23:1–3

_____

_____

_____

_____

_____

Leviticus 19:15

_____

_____

_____

_____

Proverbs 18:5

_____

_____

_____

_____

_____

Acts 10:34–35

_____

_____

_____

_____

Romans 2:11

_____

_____

_____

_____

Galatians 2:6

_____

_____

_____

_____

Ephesians 6:9

_____

_____

_____

_____

_____

1 Timothy 5:21

_____

_____

_____

_____

_____

WEEK 3, DAY 5

James and Our World Today

When we look at the theme of favoritism in James, it can become the lens through which we see ourselves, our world, and how God works in our world today.

1. How does the command in James not to show favoritism affect how we see our world, God's action, and ourselves in our world today?

Our world constantly shows favoritism to the wealthy, the beautiful, and the articulate. This is what we see in the media, so the principle of showing favoritism sneaks into our thinking without us even being aware of it. As Christians, we need to be constantly aware that God sees people differently from the world, and we should too. God will judge us for showing favoritism.

Following the above example, answer these questions about how we can understand ourselves, our world, and God's action in our world today.

2. How has favoritism in our world skewed what we value?

_____

_____

_____

_____

_____

3. How can we protect and support the marginalized in our societies today, and what is the difference between showing mercy (or protection) and showing partiality, as the Exodus and Leviticus scriptures from Day 4 this week warn against?

_____

_____

_____

_____

_____

4. Which neighbors who are not like us are we called to love as we love ourselves in our world today?

_____

_____

_____

_____

_____

Invitation and Response

God's Word always invites a response. Think about the way this theme of favoritism from James 2:1–13 speaks to us today. How does it invite us to respond?

James is inviting us to consider some countercultural behavior that will bestow dignity on everyone equally, rather than letting worldly achievement or material wealth determine what kind of honor someone is shown.

What is your evaluation of yourself based on any or all of the verses in James 2:1–13? How might you tweak your behavior in the world today to be more in line with James's suggestions and instructions?

_____

_____

_____

_____

_____

_____

_____

_____

_____

_____

_____

_____

_____

_____

JAMES 2:14-26

The purpose of our study of James 2:14–26 is to dig more deeply into the issue that made the book of James famous: faith and deeds (or works). In chapter 2, James continues to unpack the many important ideas he has summarized in chapter 1. In this particular section, he discusses the value of a faith that does not produce good works—a faith that does not provide any outward evidence of a relationship with God.

We can discern the following pattern in the organization of these verses:

1. Faith without actions is dead ("Faith by itself, if it is not accompanied by action, is dead").

2. We demonstrate our faith by our actions. ("I will show you my faith by my deeds").

3. Examples of faith that saves ("Was not Abraham considered righteous . . . ? Was not even Rahab the prostitute considered righteous . . . ?").

53

WEEK 4, DAY 1

Absorb the passage in James 2:14–26 by reading it aloud several times until you become familiar with its verses, words, and phrases.

WEEK 4, DAY 2

The Setting

This passage builds on the previous section about showing favoritism and the emphasis on loving your neighbor as yourself. Here the emphasis is on what real, saving faith looks like on the outside. There are several concepts that the first readers and hearers would have understood and which we need to explore.

In this section, James moves from the issue of law to the issue of social concern for the neighbor's physical needs. In first-century Judaism and Christianity, the body was an important part of who a person was. Pharisaic Jews believed in the resurrection of the body, so they figured that, if God cares enough about the body to resurrect it, the body must have some connection with who a person is. The Sadducees and Romans, on the other hand, did not have concern for the body, regarding it as matter to be cast off at death and thus not part of who a person was.

The examples of faith that James uses are Abraham and Rahab. Abraham existed before the Torah was given, so his faith was evident because he did what God told him to do—most specifically, being willing to sacrifice his son Isaac to God. Rahab exemplifies the importance of hospitality. In ancient times, offering hospitality to travelers, and especially strangers, was not just a nice thing to do; it could quite literally save a person's life from bandits and illness. Rahab's hospitality resulted in the saving of the nation of Israel as it began its conquest in the land of Canaan.

The Message

To discover the message of James 2:14–26, let us look at the way the passage is structured by its writer. The author begins by giving an extreme example of concern for the physical needs of one's neighbors—they were naked and starving. Following this is an ancient debate style called a diatribe in which the author has a hypothetical opponent. Of course, the author always wins the argument and often ridicules the "opponent" for the senseless position he took. Finally, James closes this section with examples of faith in action from the scriptural tradition of his audience.

Let's examine the passage verse by verse, dividing it into eleven sections. **Below, summarize or paraphrase the general message or theme of each verse (following the pattern provided for verses 14, 15–16, and 26).**

1. James 2:14

What is the usefulness of a faith that does not result in making the world a better place?

Does this kind of faith really reveal a saving faith?

2. James 2:15–16

If a fellow human being is without the most basic necessities of life and all we offer are words of

encouragement, what good does that do them, and how does it demonstrate our faith?

3. James 2:17

4. James 2:18

5. James 2:19

_____

_____

_____

_____

_____

_____

6. James 2:20

_____

_____

_____

_____

_____

_____

7. James 2:21

_____

_____

_____

_____

_____

_____

8. James 2:22–23

_____

_____

_____

_____

_____

_____

9. James 2:24

_____

_____

_____

_____

_____

_____

10. James 2:25

_____

_____

_____

_____

_____

_____

11. James 2:26
Just as you can tell that a body is dead because there is no spirit of life in it, so faith without actions is also dead and useless.

_____

_____

_____

_____

_____

_____

What's Happening in the Passage?

As we notice the emphasis of faith evidenced by action in this passage, we will begin to see how James's first-century view is similar to or different from the realities of our world. The passage will become the lens through which we see the world in which we live today. In our study today, you may encounter words and/or phrases that are unfamiliar to you. Some of the particular words and translation choices for them have been explained in more detail in the **Word Study Notes**. If you are interested in even more help or detail, you can supplement this study with a Bible dictionary or other Bible study resource.

WORD STUDY NOTES #1

[1] The grammar used in the question indicates that he wants his hearers to think about the question. This question was also asked by the pagan philosophers who were concerned about behavior that shapes one's character versus simply a statement of beliefs.

[2] The OT prophets, John the Baptist, and Jesus all condemned religious piety without justice for the poor, giving to those in need, or doing the will of God. Even Paul, who is famous for justification by faith, emphasizes "obedience that comes from faith" (Romans 1:5).

58

1. James 2:14

James begins this section by asking a thought-provoking question.[1] What is the benefit of a faith that does not make the world a better place?[2] Can this kind of inactive faith really exhibit a faith that saves?

2. James 2:15–16

_____

_____

_____

_____

_____

3. James 2:17

_____

_____

_____

_____

_____

4. James 2:18[1]

_____

_____

_____

_____

_____

_____

_____

5. James 2:19[1]

_____

_____

_____

_____

_____

_____

_____

6. James 2:20[1,2]

_____

_____

_____

_____

_____

_____

_____

WORD STUDY NOTES #4

[1]This verse begins the diatribe between an imaginary opponent and James. The opponent separates faith and works, but James sees them as a unit. You cannot have one without the other.

WORD STUDY NOTES #5

[1] The declaration that God is one is the familiar first point of the most important prayer in Judaism—the Shema. God is one. The demons also believe that God is one, but they do not do the will of God and are thus afraid of the judgment of God.

WORD STUDY NOTES #6

[1] James uses two common phrases in diatribe style. One is a direct address to the imaginary opponent: "You foolish person!" And the second is a question.

[2] The word translated "useless" in the NIV is actually "barren" in the best manuscripts. Some scribes found this term unusual and changed it to "dead," since James uses "dead" in verse 17. However, other scholars believe that James may have been making a play on words with "action" and "barren," since the roots of these words in Greek are different by only one vowel.

WORD STUDY NOTES #7

[1] Abraham was *the* example of a righteous person in Jewish tradition. The translation "was considered righteous" is a divine passive, meaning that God was the one who considered Abraham righteous because of his actions.

[2] Scholars see this justification by actions the same as justification by faith as taught by Paul—because Abraham's actions revealed his faith.

WORD STUDY NOTES #8

[1] James refers directly to Genesis 15:6 and 2 Chronicles 20:7 to confirm his position that Abraham's actions resulted in him being credited with righteousness.

[2] To be a friend of someone meant that the two of you held the same values. Here Abraham was a friend of God and not a friend of the world because he had the same values as God.

WORD STUDY NOTES #10

[1] Some ancient manuscripts translated the original word, *angelous* (angels) as "spies," since *angelos* can mean either "messenger" or "angel."

[2] Rahab gave hospitality to these spies at risk to her own life, if her actions were found out by the Jericho leadership.

7. James 2:21[1]

_____

_____

_____

_____

_____

_____

8. James 2:22-23

You can see that Abraham's faith was demonstrated in his actions—his obedience to God. His faith became mature when he acted on it. So we see that the scripture was fulfilled that said, "Abraham believed in God"—as was exhibited by his obedience—"and it was credited to him as righteousness."[1] This was a saving faith. Abraham became a friend of God—having the same values as God.[2]

9. James 2:24

From this you understand that a person has saving faith when it is demonstrated by good and obedient actions.

10. James 2:25[1,2]

_____

_____

_____

_____

_____

_____

_____

11. James 2:26

As the life-giving spirit animates the body, so good works are evidence of a living faith. Faith without the evidential works is dead.

Discoveries

Let's summarize our discoveries from James 2:14–26.

1. Living, saving faith will do something about a situation in which people need help—especially in matters of life and death.

2. Christianity is not just about learning to *say* the right thing at the right time; it is also about *doing* the right thing at the right time.

3. Merely believing in correct doctrine is not evidence of having a saving faith. It must be expressed by obedient action.

4. The best way to mature our faith is to do what God asks us to do.

5. To show that we are friends of God rather than friends of the world, we need to demonstrate that we hold the same values as God.

6. Showing hospitality to strangers is one of the values of God. Strangers (or immigrants) represent a class of people who are vulnerable in society.

7. If we want to be revived in our faith, one sure way is to obediently do what God tells us to do. We do not need to wait to hear the voice of God. God has already communicated his will in Scripture.

Faith, Actions, and the Story of God

If you have a study Bible, it may have references in a margin, a middle column, or footnotes that point to other biblical texts. You may find it helpful in understanding how the whole story of God ties together to look up some of those other scriptures from time to time. Whenever we read a biblical text, it is important to ask how the particular text we are reading relates to the rest of the Bible. The theme of faith exhibited and made mature by actions has an important place in the story of God. This theme is found in several places in the Bible in a variety of contexts. In the Old and New Testaments, the theme of faith and actions is common. The Bible often gives direction and advice to God's people on right action. **In the space given below, write a short summary of how the theme of faith and action is discussed in each passage.**

Genesis 22:1–18

_____

_____

_____

_____

_____

Joshua 2:1–21; 6:22–25

_____

_____

_____

_____

_____

Amos 2:4–16

_____

_____

_____

_____

_____

Micah 6:6–8

_____

_____

_____

_____

_____

Matthew 7:17–21

_____

_____

_____

_____

_____

Matthew 25:31–46

_____

_____

_____

_____

_____

Galatians 5:22–26

_____

_____

_____

_____

_____

Colossians 1:9-12

_____

_____

_____

_____

_____

WEEK 4, DAY 5

James and Our World Today

When we look at the theme of faith and actions in James 2:14–26, this theme can become the lens through which we see ourselves, our world, and how God works in our world today.

1. What do we see when we look at ourselves and our world today through the lens of James's perspective that faith becomes mature through obedient action?

Our world drives each person to get ahead, no matter what. The world views people's actions as self-motivated—the goal is to get that next position, relationship, or promotion. Christians, on the other hand, should do what they do because of their love for God and a desire to be more Christlike. Therefore, Christians and worldly people may do the same things from time to time, but the motivations and the goals are entirely different. Christians may not gain worldly recognition, but we become more mature, Christlike people. In contrast, those who do things for their own personal gain can become hard-hearted and selfish.

Following the above example, answer these questions about how we can understand ourselves, our world, and God's action in our world today.

2. What do you observe about how faith without obedient action has affected your life and the lives of your friends?

3. What are some examples of how we can meet the emotional, physical, and social (as well as the spiritual) needs of our neighbors?

4. What is an example you have seen of mature faith acted out in good works in your community? What can we do to encourage this kind of active, mature faith?

_____

_____

_____

_____

_____

Invitation and Response

God's Word always invites a response. Think about the way this theme of faith and actions from James 2:14–26 speaks to us today. How does it invite us to respond?

God's Word has given us a blueprint for obedience. We must pray for an openness to God's nudging in our lives and the opportunities the Holy Spirit gives us to do good works.

_____

_____

_____

_____

65

What is your evaluation of yourself based on any or all of the verses found in James 2:14–26?

_____

_____

_____

_____

_____

_____

_____

_____

_____

_____

Abraham became a friend of God—having the same values as God.

JAMES 3

The purpose of our study of James 3 is to discover the role of the tongue in revealing true character. James closes this chapter with a section on earthly and heavenly wisdom, which the tongue certainly plays a part in proclaiming. In chapter 3, James continues to unpack the many important ideas he summarized in chapter 1. In this particular section, he develops the idea of faith expressed in good actions by concentrating on what comes out of our mouth. Good works or actions are not limited to what we may do with our hands; they are related to what we say and how we say it.

We can discern the following pattern in the organization of these verses:

1. Teachers are held to a higher standard ("We who teach will be judged more strictly").

2. The tongue has a lot of power ("It is a restless evil, full of deadly poison").

3. Good and bad things come out of the same mouth ("Out of the same mouth come praise and cursing").

4. Earthly and heavenly wisdom are seen in daily life ("Let them show [their wisdom] by their good life, by deeds done in the humility that comes from wisdom").

WEEK 5, DAY 1

Absorb the passage in James 3 by reading it aloud several times until you become familiar with its verses, words, and phrases.

WEEK 5, DAY 2

The Setting

This passage builds on the previous faith and actions section but concentrates on both the good and bad that can be done by the tongue. Here, the emphasis is on what real saving faith looks like in what we say. There are several concepts we need to explore that the first readers and hearers would have understood.

Teachers in the first century were highly regarded. "Teacher" is an appropriate translation of the Jewish title "Rabbi." In Jewish and Christian traditions of the first and second centuries, teaching was considered a divine office. Jews saw teachers as the successors of the prophets, and scholars think that teaching was the primary role of pastors in the early church.

Teaching in the Hellenistic context meant presenting material in a systematic way. Therefore, being able to use language accurately to communicate significant ideas was extremely important. Additionally, within the Christian context, we find an emphasis on the behavior of the teacher indicating whether they are true or false teachers.

Teachers were associated with the idea of wisdom. There is an important section of the Old Testament—called The Writings—that contains the Wisdom books. James is considered the only Wisdom book in the New Testament. There are, of course, references to Wisdom and wisdom sayings throughout the New Testament, but James, with his ethical emphasis, captures the heart of *Jewish* wisdom for the New Testament.

Jewish Wisdom literature is concerned with how one lives a godly life in a fallen world. Proverbs 9:10 and Psalm 111:10 affirm that the fear of God is the beginning of wisdom. The difference between earthly and heavenly wisdom was an important distinction in the first century, since Greek (or Hellenistic) philosophy was widely known.

The Message

To discover the message of James 3, let us examine the passage verse by verse, dividing it into eleven sections. **Below, summarize or paraphrase the general message or theme of each verse or grouping of verses (following the pattern provided for verses 1–2, 3–4, and 18).**

1. James 3:1–2

Not many should aspire to be teachers because teachers are (were) held to a very high standard.

All of us fail at different things, but people who can control their tongues are mature and are

able to also control all their thoughts and actions.

2. James 3:3–4

We can control horses by putting a small bit in their mouth. One pull on the reins and we can

turn the whole animal around. A very small rudder also controls large ships. All the captain needs

to do is turn the rudder and the ship goes wherever the captain wants to go.

3. James 3:5–6

4. James 3:7–8

5. James 3:9

_____

_____

_____

_____

_____

6. James 3:10

_____

_____

_____

_____

_____

7. James 3:11–12

_____

_____

_____

_____

_____

8. James 3:13

_____

_____

_____

_____

_____

9. James 3:14–16

_____

_____

_____

_____

_____

10. James 3:17

_____

_____

_____

_____

_____

11. James 3:18
Peacemakers bring about peace by seeing that justice and fairness happen in the community.

_____

_____

_____

_____

_____

_____

WEEK 5, DAY 3

What's Happening in the Passage?

As we notice the emphasis of faith as demonstrated by what we say, we will begin to see how James's first-century view is similar to or different from the realities of our world. The passage will become the lens through which we see the world in which we live today. In our study today, you may encounter words and/or phrases that are unfamiliar to you. Some of the particular words and translation choices for them have been explained in more detail in the **Word Study Notes**. If you are interested in even more help or detail, you can supplement this study with a Bible dictionary or other Bible study resource.

WORD STUDY NOTES #1

[1] Teachers were highly respected in the first century, and so those craving respect were often tempted to become teachers. Teachers not only needed a good command of language but were also judged by their lifestyles. Early Christians judged whether a person was a true or false teacher by the teacher's actions.

1. James 3:1–2

James begins this section by making a surprising statement to his fellow believers, his readers. He cautions them not to aspire to be teachers because teachers are held to a higher standard.[1] We all have our faults, but the person who can control his or her tongue is certainly mature and able to control all thoughts and actions.

Practice the above pattern to summarize verses 3–4.

2. James 3:3–4

_____

_____

_____

_____

_____

_____

_____

3. James 3:5-6

Like the bit in the horse's mouth or the rudder for the ship, the tongue is a small part of the body, but it has great power—for good or ill. As in verse 2, the one who is able to control the tongue has the restraint and maturity needed to control all of their actions. Also, a very small flame—even just a "spark," says James—can turn into a wild forest fire. In the same way, an uncontrolled tongue can do a lot of damage, both to others and to oneself. The damage done often follows one to the grave.

4. James 3:7-8[1]

_____

_____

_____

_____

_____

_____

WORD STUDY NOTES #4

[1] The word translated "restless" means "unstable" and may be a reference to the double-minded or double-souled person from James 1:8. Poisons were well-known ways of getting rid of rivals, or of dying by suicide.

73

5. James 3:9

Not only are tongues unstable and deadly, but they are also used in hypocritical ways: both to praise God and to curse the human beings who were created in God's own image.[1]

6. James 3:10

_____

_____

_____

_____

_____

_____

_____

WORD STUDY NOTES #5

[1] The word translated "praise" can also be translated "bless," but it is a different Greek word than the one used in the Beatitudes. The word used here means to speak well of someone, but it is momentary, emphasizing the instability of the tongue.

74

7. James 3:11–12[1]

_____

_____

_____

_____

_____

_____

_____

8. James 3:13

James says that the "wise and understanding"[1] can demonstrate[2] their knowledge and maturity by their humble, Christlike life-styles.[3]

9. James 3:14–16

If you are a bitter fanatic about what you know or have selfish ambition, do not boast about your expertise and intelligence or live a life that denies the gospel. This kind of "wisdom" is worldly, unspiritual, and of the devil. For where there is fanaticism and selfish ambition, there you will find instability and morally abhorrent actions.

10. James 3:17[1, 2, 3, 4, 5]

_____

_____

_____

_____

_____

_____

_____

11. James 3:18

God raises a harvest of justice, righteousness, and peace for those who seek to make peace.[1]

Discoveries

Let's summarize our discoveries from James 3.

1. Teachers are held to a higher standard when it comes to the use of words. This higher standard is not just in their command of vocabulary but also in living a life that is consistent with what is taught.

2. Although the tongue is a very small part of the body, it is the most difficult part to control. If we can control our tongue, we can control our whole selves.

3. An uncontrolled tongue can damage not just the person spoken to but also the speaker. A wicked tongue can cause trouble that will follow a person to the grave.

4. It is useless to try to disguise what is in our hearts, at the core of our being, because it will eventually come out in what we say and do.

5. Godly words and actions come from godly people.

WORD STUDY NOTES #10

[1] James contrasts the two earthly wisdom vices ("envy and selfish ambition") with eight heavenly wisdom virtues. In Greek list structure, the first on the list is usually the most important, with the last of the list being the second-most important. It seems that James may be indicating the most important virtues as pure, peace-loving, and sincere.

[2] The word translated "pure" is from the same root as "holy."

[3] The word translated "considerate" means tolerant and easy to live with.

[4] The word translated "submissive" could be understood today as someone who is a team player.

[5] The word translated "sincere" means without hypocrisy.

WORD STUDY NOTES #11

[1] This verse is grammatically difficult, so several different translations have been suggested. It most likely is an allusion to Jesus's Beatitude in Matthew 5:9.

6. Those who are truly wise will be considerate of everyone and live morally good lives.

7. Those who are wise by heavenly standards have pure character, are peace-loving, considerate of others, are team players, exhibit mercy and good actions, do not play favorites, and are not hypocrites.

WEEK 5, DAY 4

Wisdom, Controlling the Tongue, and the Story of God

If you have a study Bible, it may have references in a margin, a middle column, or footnotes that point to other biblical texts. You may find it helpful in understanding how the whole story of God ties together to look up some of those other scriptures from time to time. Whenever we read a biblical text, it is important to ask how the particular text we are reading relates to the rest of the Bible. The themes of wisdom and controlling the tongue have an important place in the story of God. These themes are found in several places in the Bible in a variety of contexts. In the Old and New Testaments, the themes of wisdom and control of speech are common. The Bible often gives direction and advice to God's people on right action. **In the space given below, write a short summary of how these themes appear in each passage.**

Psalm 12

_____

_____

_____

_____

_____

Psalm 37:30–31

_____

_____

_____

_____

_____

Proverbs 9:9–12

_____

_____

_____

_____

_____

Proverbs 12:13–19

_____

_____

_____

_____

_____

Matthew 15:10–20

_____

_____

_____

_____

_____

Luke 21:12–15

_____

_____

_____

_____

_____

1 Corinthians 1:20–31

_____

_____

_____

_____

_____

1 Peter 3:8–12

_____

_____

_____

_____

_____

WEEK 5, DAY 5

James and Our World Today

When we look at the themes of wisdom and speech in James 3, they can become the lens through which we see ourselves, our world, and how God works in our world today.

1. What do we see when we look at ourselves and our world through the lens of James's perspective that our tongue is uncontrollable except by God?

Our world believes that one can be trained to speak well, to interview well, and to communicate well through all kinds of printed media. But only God can transform people so that what they write and speak is full of kindness, mercy, and truth.

Following the above example, answer these questions about how we can understand ourselves, our world, and God's action in our world today.

2. What have you observed about the higher standard that people are held to in this world? Who is typically held to a higher standard in our world, and why?

3. How has an uncontrolled tongue made a big impact in our world, whether historically or presently?

4. What is an example in our world today of hypocrisy—praising God but saying or doing other things that appear to contradict the gospel of Jesus Christ?

_____

_____

_____

_____

_____

5. What is the difference between earthly wisdom and heavenly wisdom, according to James, and how does that distinction show itself in our world today?

_____

_____

_____

_____

_____

Invitation and Response

God's Word always invites a response. Think about the way the themes of godly wisdom and speech from James 3 speak to us today. How do they invite us to respond?

James invites us to allow God to order our thoughts and the motivations of our hearts, which will make us wise and mature, and will lead us into merciful, edifying, gracious speech that will build up the character of others rather than tear it down. James warns us of the dangers of letting our thoughts and words go unchecked. Words and actions can never be taken back, so treating them with appropriate care is a sign of spiritual wisdom.

What is your evaluation of yourself based on any or all of the verses found in James 3?

_____

_____

_____

_____

_____

JAMES 4

The purpose of our study of James 4 is to explore some different aspects of navigating our relationships with each other and our own desires. James begins this section by referring to the problem of desires that he already introduced in 1:14. Then he builds on it by expanding on the double-souled concept he introduced in 1:8. The answer to both of these problems, he says, is humility before God. Then the topic is abruptly changed to judgment of our neighbor—particularly a brother or sister in Christ. The chapter ends with an encouragement to readers to include God in their plans.

We can discern the following pattern in the organization of these verses:

1. The double-minded need to humble themselves before God ("humble yourselves before the Lord, and he will lift you up").

2. Do not judge other Christians ("who are you to judge your neighbor?").

3. Do not boast about tomorrow ("instead, you ought to say, 'If it is the Lord's will, we will live and do this or that'").

WEEK 6, DAY 1

Absorb the passage in James 4 by reading it aloud several times until you become familiar with its verses, words, and phrases.

WEEK 6, DAY 2

The Setting

This passage builds on topics covered in chapter 1. It explores further the ideas of double-mindedness, the role of human desire, humility, why judgment of fellow Christians is a problem, and why God matters to our life's plans.

Stoicism, the most influential type of Greek philosophy in the first century, had some tenets that are helpful for Christians. Stoics believed that ethics are central to a good life and that, although we cannot change what happens to us, we can control our attitudes. They believed that the way to be happy was to develop the virtue of temperance, or moderation. The secret was to control one's desires, which is where the similarities between James and Stoicism end. Whereas Stoics believed a person had to do this all on their own, James believes that God gives us the power to do it if we humble ourselves before God.

Throughout the Old Testament, Israel is referred to as the bride of God, and when Israel rebels or strays from God's commandments, it is referred to as an adulteress. In the New Testament, the church is called the bride of Christ, with similar implications as found in the Old Testament.

In the Jewish apocalyptic literature of the intertestamental period—which is what Christians call the period between the final writings of the Old Testament canon and the first writings of the New Testament—we find the idea that if one loves God, they hate the world, and vice versa. There is no middle ground. This concept would not have been new to James's audience.

We tend to use jealousy and envy interchangeably in English, but in the Greek philosophical context, there is a distinct difference between these two words. Jealousy is considered a positive emotion because it encourages people to better themselves so they can have what the person they are jealous of has. Envy is always a negative emotion because it means that the person who is envious wants to do harm to the one they envy so they can get what the other has. As a result, people tried to protect themselves from envy. Some used protective charms, but most often they were warned not to boast about what they had. Boasting was not only avoided because it made the boaster look proud but also because it invited envy, which could do harm to the boaster.

The first-century society was an agricultural society where land ownership was the basis of wealth. The wealthy person had a country home and primary residence on the land they owned, but they also had a city house where they lived on a part-time basis, received their clients, met with employees, and conducted business. Therefore, the cities were primarily market centers where merchants brought their wares to sell. We know Paul and many of his associates were artisans who made and sold their items in the cities. It is likely that many early Christians were from this level of society, so planning trips to new markets (cities) would be a common business strategy.

The Message

To discover the message of James 4, let's examine the passage verse by verse, dividing it into eleven sections. **Below, summarize or paraphrase the general message or theme of each verse or grouping of verses (following the pattern provided for verses 1–2 and 3).**

1. James 4:1–2

Fights and quarrels among Christians spring from our desires. These desires can cause us to do bad things because of our envy and jealousy. One reason we do not have what we want is that we don't ask God for it.

2. James 4:3

Another reason we do not get what we want is that, when we do ask God for something, we ask with the wrong (self-serving) motives.

3. James 4:4–5

4. James 4:6

_____

_____

_____

_____

_____

_____

5. James 4:7–8

_____

_____

_____

_____

_____

_____

6. James 4:9–10

_____

_____

_____

_____

_____

_____

7. James 4:11–12

_____

_____

_____

_____

_____

_____

8. James 4:13

_____

_____

_____

_____

_____

_____

9. James 4:14–15

_____

_____

_____

_____

_____

_____

10. James 4:16

_____

_____

_____

_____

_____

_____

11. James 4:17

_____

_____

_____

_____

_____

_____

WEEK 6, DAY 3

WORD STUDY NOTES #1

[1] The word translated "desires" actually has a stronger meaning of "sensual pleasures." These sensual pleasures are doing battle within the person.

[2] Scholars have debated whether James actually meant that Christians were killing other Christians. While it seems extreme to us today, murder is often paired with envy in ancient literature, and it is true that Christians have killed other Christians over power struggles and differences in theology.

[3] The verb tense being used in verse 2 with "ask" uses the Greek middle voice, which indicates that the asking is for their own benefit.

What's Happening in the Passage?

As we notice certain emphases in the passage, we will begin to see how James's first-century view is similar to or different from the realities of our world. The passage will become the lens through which we see the world in which we live today. In our study today, you may encounter words and/or phrases that are unfamiliar to you. Some of the particular words and translation choices for them have been explained in more detail in the **Word Study Notes**. If you are interested in even more help or detail, you can supplement this study with a Bible dictionary or other Bible study resource.

1. James 4:1–2

This chapter begins following the last verse of chapter 3, where James praises peacemakers. The divisions and fights in the church are due to people's selfish desires.[1] Contrary to what one would expect to find in a church, Christians are murdering[2] fellow Christians and envying others because they are not getting what they want, and they are not getting what they want because they are not asking (or seeking) God.[3]

2. James 4:3

_____

_____

_____

_____

_____

_____

3. James 4:4–5

When James calls them "adulterous people,"[1] he is making a reference to their unfaithfulness as the people of God. Whoever chooses to be a friend of the world cannot be a friend of God[2] because their values are completely opposite. Scripture tells us that the spirit (life force) God caused to live in us envies intensely.[3]

4. James 4:6[1]

_____

_____

_____

_____

_____

_____

_____

WORD STUDY NOTES #3

[1] The phrase translated "You adulterous people" is simply "adulteresses" in the Greek because readers would have identified themselves with Israel, who was the bride of God.

[2] In the first century, a "friend" was someone who held the same status and values. The world and God do not hold the same values, so a "friend of God" (having the same values) cannot be a friend of the world. These are mutually exclusive.

[3] Verse 5 is notoriously difficult to translate. The formula "Scripture says" would indicate that James is quoting Scripture, but what comes next is not found in canonical Scripture. The grammar is also ambiguous. Therefore, interpretation is left to context. Since envy is always used negatively and never in reference to God, we should not interpret this passage to say that God enviously longs for the spirit. It must be the spirit within Christians that envies, an idea that also agrees with what was said in verse 2.

WORD STUDY NOTES #4

[1] The end of verse 6 is a nearly exact quote from Proverbs 3:34 in the Septuagint (the Greek translation of the Old Testament).

WORD STUDY NOTES #5

[1] The translation here is fairly straightforward, but there are a couple of issues. First, in chapter 1, James tells us that our desires lead to sin, but here we find James, in agreement with the rest of the gospel tradition, saying that the devil is behind our evil desires. Secondly, purity is also identified with single-mindedness and so is a good contrast to double-mindedness.

WORD STUDY NOTES #7

[1] "Slander" is understood to be the result of envy, which is breaking the commandments.

[2] Verse 12 uses the same structure as 2:19, with "one" being placed first in the sentence, to indicate the importance of the idea that God alone can judge.

5. James 4:7–8[1]

_____

_____

_____

_____

_____

6. James 4:9–10

_____

_____

_____

_____

_____

7. James 4:11–12[1,2]

_____

_____

_____

_____

8. James 4:13

James is now specifically addressing those who make their livelihood traveling around to different cities to sell their wares or ply their trades.

9. James 4:14–15[1]

_____

_____

_____

_____

_____

WORD STUDY NOTES #9

[1] The word translated "know" in verse 14 is not the common word for "know." It means having a thorough understanding of all the data, like an accountant who is studying all the transactions in a finance report.

10. James 4:16[1,2]

_____

_____

_____

_____

_____

WORD STUDY NOTES #10

[1] Remember that boasting is warned against because it invites envy and the harm that envy can cause.

[2] The word translated as "arrogant schemes" means to show off what a person pretends to be or have.

11. James 4:17

Here James broadens the generally accepted definition of sin from "willful wrongdoing" to include avoiding doing good things we know we should be doing.

Discoveries

Let's summarize our discoveries from James 4.

1. Conflicts among Christians come from selfish desires.

2. Christians do not get what they want because of one of two things: either they haven't asked God, or what they have asked for is not something that will benefit the kingdom.

3. Christians who have the same values as the world are in rebellion against God. No one can make both the world and God happy.

4. The only way for Christians to get right with God is to humbly submit themselves before God, actively resist the devil, and be deeply sorry for their rebellion against God.

5. Christians should not slander each other or judge each other. Only God who is the Lawgiver can be the Judge.

6. Christians need to include God in their earthly plans. God's values need to be part of every aspect of Christian lives.

7. If you are prompted to do something for God and you do not do it, that is sin.

WEEK 6, DAY 4

Human Desire and the Story of God

If you have a study Bible, it may have references in a margin, a middle column, or footnotes that point to other biblical texts. You may find it helpful in understanding how the whole story of God ties together to look up some of those other scriptures from time to time. Whenever we read a biblical text, it is important to ask how the particular text we are reading relates to the rest of the Bible. The themes of human desires and living for God have an important place in the story of God and are found in several places in the Bible in a variety of contexts. **In the space given below, write a short summary of how the themes of human desire and living for God are discussed in each passage.**

Jeremiah 3:19–22

_____

_____

_____

_____

_____

Psalm 24:3–6

_____

_____

_____

_____

_____

Proverbs 11:6

_____

_____

_____

_____

_____

Habakkuk 2:4

_____

_____

_____

_____

_____

Matthew 5:21–22

_____

_____

_____

_____

_____

Mark 8:34–38

_____

_____

_____

_____

1 Corinthians 6:1–8

_____

_____

_____

_____

_____

Philippians 2:1–4

_____

_____

_____

_____

_____

WEEK 6, DAY 5

James and Our World Today

When we look at the themes of human desires and living for God in James 4, these themes can become the lens through which we see ourselves, our world, and how God works in our world today.

1. What do we see when we look at ourselves and our world through the lens of James's perspective that conflict is caused by desire and that we should include God in our plans?

Our world claims that we should have what we desire; after all, we deserve it! However, reality

is different. If our values are God's values, then what we want is what God wants, which is not

necessarily what might make our lives easier or more fun.

_____

_____

Following the above example, answer these questions about how we can understand ourselves, our world, and God's action in our world today.

2. Is there such a thing as holy conflict? James doesn't seem to think so. He says that conflict between Christians stems from selfish desires. How do you perceive that to be true in the church and in the world today?

_____

_____

_____

_____

_____

3. Are there things you have asked God for and have not gotten? How might your desires change if God changed your heart?

_____

_____

_____

_____

_____

4. How can Christians include God in our earthly plans? How can we make God's values part of the way we pursue a livelihood?

_____

_____

_____

_____

_____

5. James tells us that if we know God wants us to do something, and we don't do it, it is sin. Why do you think he said that? Does this idea remind you of any particular story from elsewhere in the Bible?

_____

_____

_____

_____

_____

Invitation and Response

God's Word always invites a response. Think about the way the themes of human desire and living for God speak to us today. How do they invite us to respond?

When we pray and ask God to transform our hearts so that they look more like the heart of God, we may find that the things we want and the things we value begin to change. James invites us to lean fully into that change in order to become more faithful disciples.

What is your evaluation of yourself based on any or all of the verses found in James 4?

_____

_____

_____

_____

_____

No one can make
both the world
and God happy.

JAMES 5

The purpose of our study of James 5 is to understand several important issues: the role of the rich, patience in the suffering of the poor, swearing, the prayer of faith, and turning the wandering Christian back to God. James begins this section by expanding on the woes of the rich, which he introduced in chapter 1. Then he turns to encourage the poor as they wait for justice. Next, he abruptly changes the topic to speaking simply and truthfully so that swearing or oaths are not necessary. Then he spends five verses encouraging the actions that will build and care for the community. Finally, he ends chapter 5 by encouraging his readers to go after the brothers and sisters who have wandered from the truth and bring them back to the community.

We can discern the following pattern in the organization of these verses:

1. The warning to the corrupt rich ("rich people, weep and wail because of the misery that is coming on you").

2. Patience in suffering ("be patient and stand firm, because the Lord's coming is near").

3. Do not swear ("do not swear—not by heaven or by earth or by anything else").

4. Dealing with trouble, happiness and illness in the church ("Is anyone among you in trouble? . . . happy? . . . sick?").

5. Bringing back the wanderer ("if one of you should wander from the truth . . .").

WEEK 7, DAY 1

Absorb the passage in James 5 by reading it aloud several times until you become familiar with its verses, words, and phrases.

WEEK 7, DAY 2

The Setting

This passage builds on some topics covered in chapter 1 and adds a few community-related topics. Chapter 5 explores further the ideas of the corrupt rich, patience in suffering, oaths, prayer, and turning the wandering Christian back to the truth.

In English and for the modern reader, we add "corrupt" to the word "rich" in James. There is no such adjective in the Greek text because first-century readers would have already understood that the rich were corrupt based on their historical, cultural, and religious contexts. As we've discussed in previous chapters, the rich had historically oppressed the poor by not giving them their appropriate wages. The Old Testament prophets Amos, Micah, and Isaiah all call out the rich for their oppression of the poor. Therefore, the corruption was a long-standing practice.

Culturally, Jews and early Christians believed that there was just enough of everything—food, water, health, fertility, etc.—for everyone to have what they needed. Therefore, since the rich had more than they needed, that must mean they had taken from others who did not have enough. Religiously, the rich had also compromised themselves with the Syrian empire in the two hundred years before Christ's birth in order to gain economic advantage. The poor rebelled against the Syrians in the Maccabean Revolt of the 160s BC. They set up the Hasmonean Dynasty, which ruled Palestine for eighty years before the Romans took over.

Finally, in Luke 6, Jesus blesses the poor, "for [theirs] is the kingdom of God" (v. 20). This scripture led to further assumptions of "poor" meaning "righteous" and "rich" meaning "corrupt." Although this may not have been the reality in every individual case, it was the generalized assumption based on economic status.

For the Jews, the last days begin with the appearance of the Messiah. Therefore, the readers of James considered themselves to be living in the last days, which is why James urges the poor to be patient—because judgment would soon come for their oppressors. Job is mentioned because he is the prominent example in Jewish literature of someone who was patient in suffering. And, just as Job is the example of patience, Elijah is the example of a person who prayed and got tangible results. We find these stories in our Old Testament, but they also appear in the apocryphal books and in the oral tradition of the rabbis.

Olive oil had many uses in Jewish tradition, from anointing someone to be king, to preparing food, to being used as a medicine. So James is encouraging both prayer and medical attention when confronting illness in the community.

In both James and in Jesus's ministry we see the apparently widespread understanding that a person's spiritual condition and physical condition are interrelated (see Matthew 9, Mark 2, and Luke 5). The Jews believed in the holistic nature of a person. While the Greeks divided the person into body and spirit or body, soul, and spirit (See 1 Thessalonians 5:23 and 2 Corinthians 7:1 for examples in Paul's letters), the Jews understood that one could not separate the body out into different parts. Therefore, what was happening to the spirit was also happening to the body. This is also important for understanding James's insistence that what one truly believes will come out in one's actions.

The Message

To discover the message of James 5, let us examine the passage verse by verse, dividing it into eleven sections. **Below, summarize or paraphrase the general message or theme of each verse or grouping of verses (following the pattern provided for verses 1 and 2–3).**

1. James 5:1

The rich are to weep and cry because their easy life is coming to an end and they will soon be miserable.

2. James 5:2–3

Instead of using their wealth for good purposes, they have only hoarded it. As a result, their wealth is now, or soon will be, worthless, and it convicts them of greed and insensitivity to the poor.

3. James 5:4–6

_____
_____
_____
_____
_____
_____

4. James 5:7–8

_____
_____
_____
_____
_____
_____

5. James 5:9

_____
_____
_____
_____
_____
_____

6. James 5:10–11

_____
_____
_____
_____
_____

7. James 5:12

_____

_____

_____

_____

_____

_____

8. James 5:13

_____

_____

_____

_____

_____

_____

9. James 5:14–16

_____

_____

_____

_____

_____

_____

10. James 5:17–18

_____

_____

_____

_____

_____

_____

11. James 5:19–20

WEEK 7, DAY 3

What's Happening in the Passage?

As we notice the emphases of warning the rich, comforting the poor, and giving directions for community life, we will begin to see how James's first-century view is similar to or different from the realities of our world. The passage will become the lens through which we see the world in which we live today. In our study today, you may encounter words and/or phrases that are unfamiliar to you. Some of the particular words and translation choices for them have been explained in more detail in the **Word Study Notes**. If you are interested in even more help or detail, you can supplement this study with a Bible dictionary or other Bible study resource.

1. James 5:1

This verse immediately follows the end of chapter 4, where James is talking to merchants and tradespeople about how they conduct their business and include God in their plans. Perhaps some of those addressed in the previous section can be counted as rich, but more likely this is a major subject change. James is warning those who have been corrupt or dishonest with their wealth that the coming judgment will bring them misery.[1] He is not so much commanding them to cry ("weep and wail")[2] about it as simply warning them that it is going to happen.

2. James 5:2–3

James's words in these verses are not so much describing current reality but the reality that James believes the judgment will bring. Wealth will be as useful against the judgment as if it had rotted,[1] corroded (or rusted), and it will be as if their own flesh is on fire.[2] The corrosion of wealth at the judgment will prove that they did not use their position to help others. The age of Jesus (the Messiah) ushered in "the last days," which means they know judgment is coming, but they still chose to hoard more than they needed.

WORD STUDY NOTES #1

[1] The word translated "misery" comes most likely from Isaiah and indicates the result of judgment by God.

[2] The word translated "weep" is an outward expression of sorrow and is associated with repentance in the gospels (see Matthew 26:75 and Luke 7:38). The word "wail" occurs only here in the Greek New Testament but is probably influenced by Isaiah's use to mean "howl." This Greek word is also found in pagan sources. It means to "cry aloud" or "shriek."

WORD STUDY NOTES #2

[1] The word translated "rotted" is used in cases of rotting fruits and vegetables, which may indicate that the wealth of these people was agricultural.

[2] The terms "corroded" and "fire" are often used in apocalyptic contexts, indicating again that James is referring to the last days.

3. James 5:4–6[1, 2, 3, 4, 5]

_____

_____

_____

_____

_____

_____

_____

_____

_____

_____

_____

_____

WORD STUDY NOTES #3

[1] The verb translated "failed to pay" in verse 4 indicates a meaning of willful stealing rather than a simple oversight.

[2] "Lord Almighty" emphasizes the power of God to do anything to anyone.

[3] The word in verse 5 translated "self-indulgence" means to spend wealth on oneself beyond the limits of propriety. If applied to eating and drinking, it means they ate until it made them sick. This contrasts with the fact that, because the workers were not paid the wages they were due, they were going hungry.

[4] Ironically, the rich were fattening themselves for slaughter. Most commentators take "the day of slaughter" to refer to the day of judgment. However, using the term "slaughter" fits well with the idea of been fattened for slaughter.

[5] Scholars have debated the meaning of "the innocent one" who does not fight back in verse 6. Some think James means Jesus, thus making the corrupt rich the murderers of Jesus. Some think the text is referring to James himself, something added by a later editor of the epistle. Most modern commentators believe it is referring to the righteous poor. "The innocent one" is actually "the righteous one" and so fits with the first-century Jewish understanding of the nature of the poor.

4. James 5:7–8[1, 2]

_____

_____

_____

_____

_____

_____

5. James 5:9[1, 2]

_____

_____

_____

_____

_____

_____

6. James 5:10–11

James says we should imitate the prophets who proclaimed the message of God as examples of how to live patiently in the face of suffering and hardship. We consider those who have persevered[1] to be blessed by God. James knew his readers would know the story of Job and how it ended. James wants his readers to remember that the Lord is compassionate and merciful.

7. James 5:12[1]

_____

_____

_____

_____

_____

_____

_____

_____

8. James 5:13[1]

_____

_____

_____

_____

_____

_____

_____

9. James 5:14–16

In these verses, James is encouraging community participation at every turn, from anointing to prayers for healing to confession.[1]

10. James 5:17–18[1]

_____

_____

_____

_____

_____

_____

_____

_____

WORD STUDY NOTES #7

[1] While Judaism allowed oaths, Jesus forbids it in Matthew 5:34–37. This is a very close allusion to Jesus without directly quoting Jesus. This functions as a close to James's discussion on negative speech.

WORD STUDY NOTES #8

[1] The words translated as "trouble" and "happy" in the NIV come from similar roots. Both are feelings, one bad and one good.

WORD STUDY NOTES #9

[1] Because forgiveness and healing are so closely related in Jewish thought, Christians are encouraged to continually confess their sins to each other so that they might remain well and healthy.

WORD STUDY NOTES #10

[1] Elijah is described as a person with the same capacity for emotion that we have. In other words, he is an ordinary human being.

[1] In these verses there is some ambiguity about whose soul is saved from death and whose sins are forgiven or covered up. Most scholars believe that in both cases the person who wandered away and was brought back is the "sinner" being turned "from the error of their way." James does not seem very concerned with evangelism. His book is primarily about how existent Christians should develop, mature, and behave. But it is possible that in these last two verses he is showing concern for Jews who have not yet accepted Jesus as the Messiah, and that he is urging the churches to reach out to these non-Christian Jews and bring them "back" to the truth of God.

11. James 5:19–20[1]

_____

_____

_____

_____

_____

_____

Discoveries

Let's summarize our discoveries from James 5.

1. What God gives us in earthly resources we are expected to use for the benefit of others—not to squander in pampering ourselves.

2. God wants social and economic justice for all people. God will eventually judge and punish those who use their power, wealth, and influence to oppress others.

3. Christians are to wait patiently and endure the circumstances of persecution or hardship without complaining about other Christians.

4. Christians should create a loving and caring community so that those who are feeling bad or depressed can admit it and have people pray with them; so that those who are happy can sing and rejoice without feeling guilty; and so that those who are sick can find healing and wholeness.

5. There is nothing wrong with asking God in prayer for what we need. God hears and answers the petition prayers of people who are living Christlike lives.

6. Sometimes Christians wander from the truth, and when they do, we should go after them and help them to come back to the truth.

7. When people come back to God, they have been saved from spiritual death—which is not a minor issue! When wandering Christians are corrected, the reputation of the church is protected.

WEEK 7, DAY 4

Life in Community and the Story of God

If you have a study Bible, it may have references in a margin, a middle column, or footnotes that point to other biblical texts. You may find it helpful in understanding how the whole story of God ties together to look up some of those other scriptures from time to time. Whenever we read a biblical text, it is important to ask how the particular text we are reading relates to the rest of the Bible. The themes of warning the rich, comforting the poor, and directions for community life have an important place in the story of God. These themes are common and are found in several places in the Bible in a variety of contexts. **In the space given below, write a short summary of how any or all of these themes of warning the rich, comforting the poor, and giving directions for community life are discussed in each passage.**

Deuteronomy 24:14–15

_____

_____

_____

_____

1 Kings 17:1, 17–21; 18:42–45

_____

_____

_____

_____

_____

Amos 4:1–3

_____

_____

_____

_____

_____

Micah 2:1–3

_____

_____

_____

_____

_____

Matthew 5:33–37

_____

_____

_____

_____

_____

Luke 12:31–34

_____

_____

_____

_____

_____

1 Corinthians 11:27–32

_____

_____

_____

_____

_____

Colossians 1:9–12

_____

_____

_____

_____

_____

WEEK 7, DAY 5

James and Our World Today

When we look at the themes of warning the rich, comforting the poor, and giving directions for community life in James, they can become the lens through which we see ourselves, our world, and how God works in our world today.

1. What do we see when we look at ourselves and our world through the lens of James's perspective in chapter 5?

Our world encourages us to indulge ourselves because we are "worth it," but the Bible tells a different story. Instead of indulging ourselves, we are to take care of the marginalized and make sure they are treated justly. Many residents of the United States are wealthy in comparison to those living elsewhere in the world. Perhaps we should heed the warnings in James and take a look at how we spend our money. Do we use it to indulge ourselves or to help others?

2. If James had known that his words would still be read thousands of years after he wrote them, might he have had different things to say, or would he still have exhorted his audience to be patient in suffering and hardship? How can we take comfort in a statement like "the Lord's coming is near" even if we can reasonably assume that our time on earth will end before it actually occurs?

3. How is it possible to create the kind of community where the sick or depressed can come and be honest about how they are feeling or ask for healing, alongside those who are happy and rejoicing? What does it look like?

_____

_____

_____

_____

_____

_____

_____

4. James says Elijah was an ordinary person who received what he asked for from God because he was a righteous person. What does that mean, and how might it change our approach to prayer?

_____

_____

_____

_____

_____

_____

_____

5. What might it look like today to go after a Christian who has wandered from the truth?

_____

_____

_____

_____

_____

_____

_____

Invitation and Response

God's Word always invites a response. Think about the way the themes of warning the rich, comforting the poor, and directions for community life from James 5 speak to us today. How do they invite us to respond?

The Word of God in the book of James offers as much encouragement as it does warning. When we obey God and behave the way the people of God ought to behave, God will be active and responsive in our lives.

What is your evaluation of yourself based on any or all of the verses found in James 5?